C000003219

GODS
ARE
FALLEN
AND
ALL
SAFETY
GONE
A
PRAYER

SELMA
DIMITRIJEVIC

SERVING THEATRE

S F

SINCE 1830

WWW.SAMUELFRENCH.CO.UK
WWW.SAMUELFRENCH.COM

Gods Are Fallen And All Safety Gone

Copyright © 2016 by Selma Dimitrijevic
All Rights Reserved

GODS ARE FALLEN AND ALL SAFETY GONE & A PRAYER is fully protected under the copyright laws of the British Commonwealth, including Canada, the United States of America, and all other countries of the Copyright Union. All rights, including professional and amateur stage productions, recitation, lecturing, public reading, motion picture, radio broadcasting, television and the rights of translation into foreign languages are strictly reserved.

ISBN 978-0-573-13011-3

www.samuelfrench.co.uk

www.samuelfrench.com

FOR AMATEUR
PRODUCTION ENQUIRIES

UNITED KINGDOM AND WORLD
EXCLUDING NORTH AMERICA
plays@SamuelFrench-London.co.uk
020 7255 4302/01

UNITED STATES AND CANADA
info@SamuelFrench.com
1-866-598-8449

Each title is subject to availability from Samuel French,
depending upon country of performance.

CAUTION: Professional and amateur producers are hereby warned that *GODS ARE FALLEN AND ALL SAFETY GONE & A PRAYER* are subject to a licensing fee. Publication of these play does not imply availability for performance. Both amateurs and professionals considering a production are strongly advised to apply to the appropriate agent before starting rehearsals, advertising, or booking a theatre. A licensing fee must be paid whether the title is presented for charity or gain and whether or not admission is charged.

The professional rights in this play are controlled by Samuel French Ltd, 52 Fitzroy Street, London, W1T 5JR.

No one shall make any changes in this title for the purpose of production. No part of this book may be reproduced, stored in a retrieval system, or transmitted in any form, by any means, now known or yet to be invented, including mechanical, electronic, photocopying, recording, videotaping, or otherwise, without the prior written permission of the publisher. No one shall upload this title, or part of this title, to any social media websites.

The right of Selma Dimitrijevic to be identified as author of this work has been asserted in accordance with Section 77 of the Copyright, Designs and Patents Act 1988.

ABOUT THE AUTHOR

SELMA DIMITRIJEVIC

Selma is a director, writer and artistic director of Greyscale. Her plays include *Night Time* (Traverse), *Game Theory* (Traverse/ek productions, shortlisted for Meyer-Whithward Award), *Time To Go* (7:84 theatre), *Broken* (Oran Mor), *Gods Are Fallen And All Safety Gone* (Oran Mor/Greyscale), *Extremely Brief And Violent* (Theatre Science), *A Prayer* (Greyscale, Title Pending award) and *Harmless Creatures* (Greyscale/Hull Truck). Selma's plays have been performed in the UK, Croatia, Ukraine, Canada and Russia.

As a librettist her work includes *Zatopek!* (South Bank) and *Friday Afternoons* (Opera North).

Work as a translator includes plays and novels by Robert Holman, David Harrower, Susan Sontag, Dave Eggers, Salman Rushdie, Roddy Doyle, James Kelman, Zadie Smith, Monica Ali, Irvine Welsh and Barry Gifford.

As a dramaturg Selma has worked with the National Theatre Studio, Tron Theatre, Exit Theatre, Caroline Horton, RashDash and the National Theatre of Scotland.

Gods Are Fallen And All Safety Gone was first commissioned by and produced for Oran Mor's A Play, A Pie and A Pint season in 2007 with the following cast:

Selina Boyack (Daughter)
Anne Lacey (Mother)

Director **Pamela Carter**

In 2012 Almeida Theatre commissioned Greyscale Theatre Company to create a new production of the show. The cast was as follows:

Scott Turnbull (Daughter)
Sean Campion (Mother)

Directed by **Selma Dimitrijevic**
Designed by **Oliver Townsend**

In 2016 this production is still touring the UK and internationally.

For my mum, Jovanka Dimitrijevic.
Thank you.

CHARACTERS

ANNE (MOTHER)
ANNIE (DAUGHTER)

Scene 1

MOTHER's house. Front room. Her room.

There is a comfortable chair and a few blankets.

Small table near. A few mugs, newspapers, glasses, TV schedule and a pair of socks scattered around the room.

It's a comfortable, warm place.

MOTHER is in her chair, asleep.

She is holding a cup of tea.

ANNIE comes in.

She just had a nice, long bath.

ANNIE gently tries taking a cup of tea from MOTHER's hand.

MOTHER wakes up.

MOTHER Oh.

ANNIE Sorry. I didn't mean to wake you up.

MOTHER I wasn't asleep.

ANNIE Can I take the...

MOTHER I'm not done yet.

ANNIE Oh. Okay.

MOTHER Have you had your bath?

ANNIE Yes.

MOTHER Was there enough hot water?

ANNIE Yes, there was plenty.

MOTHER Did you piss in the shower again?

ANNIE No. Of course I didn't.

MOTHER I'm just asking.

ANNIE I never do that.

MOTHER It's a cunt to clean, you know.

ANNIE Sorry?

MOTHER It's hard to clean.

ANNIE Right.

MOTHER Come here.

ANNIE What?

MOTHER Come here.

> **MOTHER** *spits on her thumb and wipes* **ANNIE***'s face.*

ANNIE What is it?

MOTHER Toothpaste. There.

ANNIE Thank you.

MOTHER That's better.

ANNIE Where's Dad gone?

MOTHER How would I know? You think he tells me anything?

ANNIE He just disappeared.

MOTHER That's your dad for you.

ANNIE I wanted to talk to him.

MOTHER Maybe next time.

ANNIE Always "next time".

MOTHER What did they say about the weather?

ANNIE Who?

MOTHER On the radio.

ANNIE Some rain I think. Cloudy. Nothing too bad.

MOTHER Tz, tz, tz.

ANNIE —

    What?

MOTHER It'll kill the crops.

ANNIE Will it now?

MOTHER Oh yes.

ANNIE And what do you know about crops?

MOTHER I know what kills them.

    Rain and strong winds. Kills them. Just like that.

ANNIE It's April, mum, bit of rain is just fine.

MOTHER You'll see once they're all dead. Just you wait.

ANNIE I saw Aunt Marie this morning.

MOTHER Did you?

ANNIE Yes.

MOTHER And. Is she well?

ANNIE Well, no.

    —

    How could she be?

MOTHER What's wrong now?

ANNIE Didn't she tell you?

MOTHER Tell me what?

ANNIE Someone broke into their house.

MOTHER When?

ANNIE Last night.

MOTHER See. No one tells me anything.

ANNIE She left you a message.

MOTHER No she didn't.

ANNIE Well she said she did.

MOTHER Where?

ANNIE On your answering machine.

MOTHER Ah.

ANNIE Didn't you hear it?

MOTHER I heard the phone.

ANNIE And?

MOTHER It was ringing all bloody evening.

ANNIE So why didn't you answer it then?

MOTHER Your dad wasn't here.

ANNIE So what?

MOTHER You know I don't like answering the phone when your dad is not around. Besides, it was late, who knows who it was.

ANNIE It was Aunt Marie.

MOTHER Well I didn't know that, did I?

ANNIE Well if you answered the phone you'd know.

MOTHER I don't know. All that stuff they've got. It's just asking for trouble.

ANNIE Luckily the burglars didn't take anything.

MOTHER So why call me then in the middle of the night.

ANNIE I don't know, I think she just got a fright.

MOTHER And you went to see her?

ANNIE Yes, Mark and I stopped by this morning. You know, to see if there is anything we can do.

MOTHER Like what?

ANNIE I don't know, check if they are all right, maybe tidy up a bit.

MOTHER And you need Mark to tidy up?

ANNIE No, I didn't need him, but it was nice of him to come.

MOTHER Didn't he have to go to work?

ANNIE Mum.

MOTHER What?

ANNIE It's Sunday.

MOTHER But if it wasn't…

ANNIE –

MOTHER He does have a job to go to, doesn't he?

ANNIE No, he doesn't.

MOTHER How come?

ANNIE You know very well how come.

MOTHER Remind me.

ANNIE He's looking for a job.

MOTHER Is he?

ANNIE Yes, he is.

MOTHER Oh I don't know. He could've found one by now.

ANNIE He is looking for the right one.

MOTHER Ah.

ANNIE What?

MOTHER Can't you find someone else dear?

ANNIE Mum.

MOTHER What?

ANNIE Well, you know, I kind of like Mark.

MOTHER But he doesn't make any money.

ANNIE He made loads, and we have enough now, he's just not working at the moment, but we are fine.

MOTHER Ah.

ANNIE Trust me. We have enough.

MOTHER That place you live in…

ANNIE It's perfectly nice.

MOTHER It doesn't have a bath.

ANNIE We have a shower.

MOTHER But not a bath.

ANNIE Mum, just say it, if you mind / me taking.

MOTHER You know, sometimes I really feel sorry for you, never learned to fight for yourself, did you, and now look, poor thing, having to come all the way here...

ANNIE I'm coming to see *you*. Not to have a bath. It's just that you / always fall asleep...

MOTHER So what did she say?

ANNIE Who?

MOTHER Aunt Marie, who else. Is she happy now?

ANNIE Why would she be happy?

MOTHER Now she'll have something new to moan about.

ANNIE Mum.

MOTHER We'll never hear the end of that. I'm telling you. All she ever does is talk about herself. It's all me, me, me. You know, I don't understand that, people talking about themselves all the time.

ANNIE That's not really true mum.

MOTHER And I tell her. Don't think I don't. I tell her when she starts. That's why she doesn't like me.

ANNIE She absolutely loves you.

MOTHER So did she ask about me? About my chest?

ANNIE She was still in shock.

MOTHER Yes. I'm sure she was.

ANNIE The police were there. They can't figure out how anyone got in.

MOTHER She should just go over and ask them.

ANNIE Ask who?

MOTHER You know who.

ANNIE No... I don't.

MOTHER Them, you know, from across the street. I'm sure they are quite capable of picking a lock.

ANNIE Mum. Please.

MOTHER I'm just saying.

ANNIE They are a nice family.

MOTHER And how would you know, you don't understand a word they say. You can't even talk to them.

ANNIE They speak perfectly good English.

MOTHER When it suits them. Only when it suits them.

ANNIE I think it's time you go and see them.

MOTHER See who?

ANNIE Aunt and Uncle.

MOTHER Ah. I'm too tired.

ANNIE You could do it just fine.

MOTHER I can't.

ANNIE Why not?

MOTHER I have this...here. You know. Like it's stuck. All the time now.

Like I need to wash it down.

ANNIE Well I'm sure they would let you have some water. Or tea. Or coffee.

MOTHER Ah. (I don't know.)

ANNIE Or anything else you might want to have.

MOTHER Like it's stuck. Right here. Here. Like...ugh.

ANNIE Should you go and see a doctor then?

MOTHER What do they know?

ANNIE I don't know. More than we do?

MOTHER Nah. It's just…you know. Right here. Like glue. Here.
Makes it hard to…breathe.

ANNIE Is there anything I can do?

MOTHER No, no. It's nothing for you to worry about.

ANNIE How about tea? Would a cup of tea help a little bit?

MOTHER Oh I don't know.

ANNIE Mum.

MOTHER I don't know. Maybe.

ANNIE Yes? No?

MOTHER Only if you are making it.

ANNIE –
I am, yes.

MOTHER Oh that would be nice.

ANNIE Can I take that one?

ANNIE *tries to take a mug from* MOTHER*'s hand.*

MOTHER I'm not finished yet.

ANNIE Fine. (I'll be) back in a second.

ANNIE *leaves to make the tea.*

MOTHER And don't forget the sugar, Annie, don't forget the sugar,
yes?

MOTHER *watches* ANNIE *disappear.*

Scene 2

MOTHER *is in the chair, she fell asleep.*

She is still holding a cup of tea.

ANNIE *comes in.*

She just had a nice, long bath.

ANNIE *gently tries taking a cup of tea from* MOTHER*'s hand.*

MOTHER *wakes up.*

MOTHER Oh.

ANNIE Sorry. I didn't mean to wake you up.

MOTHER I wasn't asleep.

ANNIE Can I take the…

MOTHER I'm not done yet.

ANNIE Oh. Okay.

MOTHER Have you had your bath?

ANNIE Yes.

MOTHER Was there enough hot water?

ANNIE Yes, there was plenty.

MOTHER Did you piss in the shower again?

ANNIE No. Of course I didn't.

MOTHER I'm just asking.

ANNIE I never do that.

MOTHER It's a cunt to clean, you know.

ANNIE Mum.

MOTHER It's hard to clean, I said.

ANNIE Right.

MOTHER Come here.

ANNIE What?

MOTHER Come here.

> **MOTHER** *spits on her finger and wipes* **ANNIE***'s face.*

ANNIE What is it?

MOTHER Toothpaste. There.

ANNIE Thank you.

MOTHER That's better.

ANNIE Where's Dad gone?

MOTHER How would I know? You think he tells me anything?

ANNIE He just disappeared.

MOTHER That's your dad for you.

ANNIE I wanted to talk to him.

MOTHER Maybe next time.

ANNIE Always "next time".

MOTHER What did they say about the weather?

ANNIE Who?

MOTHER On the radio.

ANNIE Hot and clear, nothing too bad I think.

MOTHER Tz, tz, tz.

ANNIE –

What now?

MOTHER It will ruin the crops. All that sun.

ANNIE Will it now?

MOTHER Oh yes.

ANNIE And what do you know about crops?

MOTHER I know what kills them. Sun.

Sun and strong winds. Kills them. Just like that.

ANNIE It's April, mum, a bit of sunshine is just fine.

MOTHER You'll see once it's all dead. Just you wait.

ANNIE I saw Aunt Marie last night.

MOTHER Did you?

ANNIE Yes.

MOTHER And is she well?

ANNIE She is just fine.

MOTHER What's wrong?

ANNIE Nothing.

MOTHER Don't lie to me. I can tell.

ANNIE It's nothing. Really. It's all fine now.

MOTHER Finish what you started.

ANNIE –

Someone broke into their house.

MOTHER No. When?

ANNIE Last night.

MOTHER And not a word to me. Nice.

ANNIE She didn't want to worry you.

MOTHER My own sister. Never tells me anything.

ANNIE Well it's not a big deal.

MOTHER Not even a phone call.

ANNIE It was late and she knows you don't like people calling you that late at night. You probably wouldn't have answered anyway.

MOTHER Of course I would. How can you say that?

ANNIE Mum.

MOTHER Not even a phone call. My own sister.

See. No one tells me anything.

ANNIE Well no-one's hurt. And nothing was taken.

MOTHER What could be taken, they never had anything.

ANNIE Anyway. They are fine now.

MOTHER Did Mark drive you there?

ANNIE No.

–

He didn't.

MOTHER How come?

ANNIE He just didn't. All right.

MOTHER What's wrong?

ANNIE Nothing.

MOTHER I don't know. That doesn't sound like Mark.

To let you do things all on your own. Take care of your family like that…

ANNIE Mum…

MOTHER Well I'm just saying.

ANNIE I don't need him to tidy up.

MOTHER It's not about needing, it's about having someone around.

ANNIE Mark and I broke up.

MOTHER No.

ANNIE Well…yes.

MOTHER But you are crap on your own.

ANNIE Oh. Thanks for that mum.

MOTHER So. What was it?

ANNIE What do you mean?

MOTHER What did you do to him?

ANNIE I didn't do anything.

MOTHER Why did he leave you then?

ANNIE Look… It's complicated.

MOTHER How complicated could it be? He is a very nice young man. He must have had a reason to leave.

ANNIE He didn't leave. It was me.

MOTHER It was you – what?

ANNIE I broke up with him.

MOTHER No. You didn't.

ANNIE Yes I did.

MOTHER You don't just go around leaving people.

ANNIE Apparently I do.

MOTHER And why would you do that?

ANNIE I told you, it's complicated.

MOTHER Do you know how old you are?

ANNIE Yes I do. Thank you.

MOTHER And what are you going to do now? What will you do without him? What can you do without him?

ANNIE I thought you didn't like him.

MOTHER Now how can you say that?

ANNIE Well somehow I was just under the impression…

MOTHER You know, you'll never find anyone as good as him, just as long as you know that.

ANNIE I don't know about that.

MOTHER He was your last chance.

ANNIE Mum.

MOTHER He buys you that nice flat and you throw him out. Just like that.

ANNIE He didn't buy it – we did. Together. And I didn't throw him out.

MOTHER So was she happy?

ANNIE Who?

MOTHER Aunt Marie, who else. You know she never liked him that much.

ANNIE No, she liked him just fine. I think it was / you who didn't.

MOTHER Did she ask about him?

ANNIE Well...no. But she was still in shock.

MOTHER They should just go and ask him about it?

ANNIE Ask who?

MOTHER That son of theirs.

ANNIE What's he got to do with it?

MOTHER Drugs.

ANNIE Drugs what?

MOTHER He needed money for drugs.

ANNIE He is not even taking drugs.

MOTHER Don't be naive. Have you seen what he looks like?

ANNIE He is sixteen. That's what sixteen-year-olds look like.

MOTHER And those friends of his. Ah.

ANNIE I think you should go and see them.

MOTHER See who?

ANNIE Aunt and Uncle.

MOTHER No. I'm too tired.

ANNIE You could do it just fine.

MOTHER I can't.

ANNIE Why not?

MOTHER I have this...here. You know. Like it's stuck. All the time now.

Like I need to wash it down.

ANNIE Well I'm sure they would let you have some water. Or tea. Or coffee.

MOTHER Ah. (I don't know.)

ANNIE Or anything else you might want to have.

MOTHER Like it's stuck. Right here. Here. Like...ugh.

ANNIE Should you go and see a doctor then?

MOTHER What do they know?

ANNIE I don't know. More than we do?

MOTHER Nah. It's just...you know. Right here. Like glue. Here.
Makes it hard to...breathe.

ANNIE Is there anything I can do?

MOTHER No, no. It's nothing for you to worry about.

ANNIE How about tea? Would a cup of tea help a little bit?

MOTHER Oh I don't know.

ANNIE Come on, mum. Yes, no?

MOTHER Only if you are making it.

ANNIE –
I am, yes.

MOTHER Lovely.

ANNIE Can I take that one?

MOTHER I'll just finish it.

ANNIE Fine. (I'll be) back in a second.

 ANNIE *leaves.*

MOTHER And don't forget the sugar, Annie, don't forget the sugar,
yes?

 MOTHER *watches* **ANNIE** *disappear.*

Scene 3

MOTHER *is in the chair, asleep.*

She is still holding a cup of tea.

ANNIE *comes in.*

She just had a nice, long bath.

ANNIE *goes to her* MOTHER *and tries gently taking a cup of tea from her hands.*

MOTHER *wakes up.*

MOTHER Oh.

ANNIE Sorry. I didn't mean to wake you up.

MOTHER I wasn't asleep.

ANNIE Can I take the…

MOTHER I'm not done yet.

ANNIE Oh. Okay.

MOTHER Have you had your bath?

ANNIE Yes.

MOTHER Was there enough water?

ANNIE Yes, there was plenty.

MOTHER Did / you piss in.

ANNIE No.

MOTHER It's / a cunt to.

ANNIE It's a cunt to clean, oh I know.

MOTHER Watch your mouth.

ANNIE Where's Dad again?

MOTHER You think he tells me where he goes?

ANNIE Mum?

MOTHER Yes?

ANNIE Do you think he is avoiding me?

MOTHER Come here.

ANNIE *(wipes her own mouth)* I'm fine.

MOTHER Oh.

ANNIE Thank you.

MOTHER So…what did they say about the weather?

ANNIE –

MOTHER On the radio?

ANNIE They said it will be…nice.

MOTHER What do you mean nice? What kind of – nice?

ANNIE You know, kind of warmish but not too hot…there was a few drops of rain during the night but nothing too heavy, actually I think they said it might be perfect for the crops.

MOTHER Tz, tz, tz.

ANNIE Jesus fucking Christ!

MOTHER Annie.

ANNIE Tell me. What's wrong with the weather now?

MOTHER Well that can't be good, can it? You know what they say: "Till April's dead, change not a thread".

ANNIE Who says that?

MOTHER It means we could still get frost. And that's / worst.

ANNIE Worst for the crops.

MOTHER Yes, frost and strong winds.

ANNIE It kills them. Yes. Well, it's nice to know what kills them. Might come in handy one day. Thank you (very much).

MOTHER I'm just saying.

ANNIE Of course you are just saying.

MOTHER Aunt Marie would know about it.

ANNIE I bet she would.

MOTHER You should ask her about it.

ANNIE I will.

MOTHER How is she anyway?

ANNIE –

MOTHER What?

ANNIE I don't really know.

MOTHER Didn't you go to see her this week?

ANNIE No.

MOTHER Oh. You really should.

ANNIE Then I did.

MOTHER When?

ANNIE Last night.

MOTHER I hope you didn't stay late. You know they don't like people coming too late.

ANNIE Actually now when I think about it – it was this morning. I went to see them this morning.

MOTHER I hope you didn't barge in while they were having their breakfast. You know how Uncle George likes his Sunday breakfast.

ANNIE Actually, when I really think about it, when I think about it very carefully – I didn't go to see them at all. In fact I phoned last night. Just before they had their tea. At a decent time. They were very happy to talk to me. And we didn't talk for more than ah well I don't know...say five, maybe ten minutes.

MOTHER Ah. What's phone. You should really go and visit sometimes.

ANNIE –

Should I?

MOTHER Yes.

ANNIE –

Fine.

MOTHER You and Mark.

ANNIE What about me and Mark?

MOTHER You could go together.

ANNIE –

Okay.

MOTHER Couldn't you?

ANNIE I don't know. Possibly.

MOTHER Why wouldn't you?

ANNIE All sorts of reasons, mum.

MOTHER You are still together though, aren't you?

ANNIE I don't know.

Would you like us to be?

MOTHER Now what kind of question is that?

ANNIE How's your chest today?

MOTHER Ah.

ANNIE Better?

MOTHER I'm still alive.

ANNIE Oh yes you are.

MOTHER And what did she say?

ANNIE Who?

MOTHER Aunt Marie. On the phone.

ANNIE Not much.

MOTHER Is she well?

ANNIE She asked about you.

MOTHER And what did you tell her?

ANNIE She said she came to see you the other day.

MOTHER No-o.

ANNIE She did. On Monday.

MOTHER She made that up.

ANNIE She said she was standing there knocking for more than ten minutes. And nothing.

MOTHER I didn't hear anything.

ANNIE Were you home on Monday?

MOTHER Where else would I be?

ANNIE I don't know… Were you maybe having a little nap?

MOTHER You know I don't sleep during the day.

ANNIE So how come you didn't hear her?

MOTHER I'm telling you she made that up.

ANNIE Why would she do that?

MOTHER Just to annoy me. That's what she does. She never liked me.

ANNIE She is just worried about you.

MOTHER Then she should come and visit sometimes.

ANNIE Jesus mum.

MOTHER Well I can't go there, can I?

ANNIE You are not that ill.

MOTHER And how do you imagine me getting there?

ANNIE Well, you put on your coat and kind of go…that way.

MOTHER Don't be ridiculous. I can't walk all the way to theirs.

ANNIE I'll drive you.

MOTHER Oh no, thank you very much.

ANNIE What now?

MOTHER I don't like the way you drive.

ANNIE You've never seen me drive.

MOTHER I've seen you ride your bike.

ANNIE What, when I was twelve?

MOTHER Let's just say it didn't fill me with confidence.

ANNIE Fine.

MOTHER I'm just saying...

ANNIE I said fine. You don't have to.

MOTHER Annie.

ANNIE I don't care. I really don't care.

MOTHER It's just not...

ANNIE What?

MOTHER Maybe next time.

ANNIE Always "next time". What if there is no next time?

MOTHER Well I can't go just right now.

ANNIE Why not? Tell me? What's the reason now?

MOTHER I don't feel too well.

ANNIE What, is there something stuck? There?

MOTHER Why are you talking to me like that?

ANNIE I don't believe this.

MOTHER I didn't mean to upset you.

ANNIE I... I can't. You know what... I just can't, mum.
When's Dad coming home?

MOTHER I don't know. He never tells me anything. No-one does.

ANNIE I want to talk to him.

MOTHER Are you upset now?

ANNIE No.

MOTHER It's just my...

ANNIE I can't. I have to...

MOTHER Don't go.

ANNIE I need to make some tea.

MOTHER Don't go right now.

ANNIE Would you like a cup?

MOTHER If you are making it.

ANNIE Well, in fact I'm not.

MOTHER Annie please don't yell.

ANNIE Well I'm not making it.

MOTHER Why did you ask me then?

ANNIE I'm not making it for myself, but I will make it for you if you want it, that's what I'm asking, would you like a cup of tea, whether I'm making it or not. Would *you* like *me* to make you a cup of tea? It's that simple. And it's not a problem, I don't mind, and I wouldn't be asking it if it was a problem.

MOTHER –

ANNIE So?

> **MOTHER** *drops her mug of tea and it spills into her lap. She coughs a bit, there is something stuck in her throat.*

What now?

> **MOTHER** *coughs. Whatever was stuck gives a bit.*

Mum?

MOTHER I'm fine.

ANNIE What was it?

MOTHER Nothing.

ANNIE Sure?

MOTHER Yes.

ANNIE So. Tea?

MOTHER Yes please.

> **MOTHER** *hands her the mug she was holding.*

ANNIE *takes it.*

Thank you.

ANNIE You are welcome.

ANNIE *leaves to make the tea.*

Scene 4

MOTHER *is still sitting in the chair.*

She is awake.

ANNIE *comes in carrying one cup of tea.*

MOTHER Hey. There you are.

ANNIE Hi.

MOTHER Hi.

ANNIE Tea.

MOTHER That's nice.

ANNIE *doesn't give tea to* MOTHER *but sips from the mug herself.*

ANNIE I've just had a bath.

MOTHER Good.

    Was it nice?

ANNIE Yes. It was.

MOTHER Good.

ANNIE I used your salts.

MOTHER They are nice, aren't they?

ANNIE Yes.

    –

    They smell like you.

MOTHER Thank you.

ANNIE And then I had a shower.

MOTHER Was there enough hot water?

ANNIE Yes. Plenty.

MOTHER Good. Good.

ANNIE And then I had a little pee in the shower.

MOTHER Oh well that's all right. It's all just water anyway, isn't it?

ANNIE But I scrubbed.

MOTHER You didn't have to.

ANNIE And now Dad is making me breakfast.

MOTHER Were there any eggs in the fridge?

ANNIE Yes. He went to the shop.

He got us papers. And bread. Some juice.

And now we will have breakfast. The two of us.

MOTHER Oh. That's nice.

ANNIE Yes.

> **MOTHER** *smiles.*

Can I... Can I ask you something?

MOTHER Of course.

ANNIE Are you...

MOTHER Yes?

ANNIE Are you happy?

MOTHER That's a funny question.

ANNIE Why?

MOTHER I don't know.

ANNIE Are you?

MOTHER Right now?

ANNIE Yes.

MOTHER I would have to think about it.

ANNIE It's...

MOTHER –

ANNIE It's different.

MOTHER Yes.

ANNIE We talk.

MOTHER Yes.

ANNIE It's odd.

MOTHER But nice.

ANNIE But odd.

MOTHER Do you...do you mind talking?

ANNIE No, not at all. Actually, I think I really like it.

It's just...

MOTHER I know.

ANNIE I have so much to ask.

MOTHER Go on.

ANNIE No.

MOTHER Why not?

ANNIE I don't know. It's too soon.

MOTHER No. It's fine.

ANNIE Really?

MOTHER I don't know. We can try. See what happens.

Go on.

ANNIE Okay...

Why...why did you stop going to Aunt Marie's?

MOTHER She would have known. She was my sister. She would have known at once.

ANNIE You think so?

MOTHER Yes. She could always tell. (It's the) same blood.

ANNIE And you didn't want her to know?

MOTHER No.

ANNIE Why? Why didn't you want anyone to know?

MOTHER You would have just worried. All of you. And that wouldn't help anyone.

ANNIE But you knew?

MOTHER Yes.

ANNIE How long?

MOTHER A while.

ANNIE How long mum?

MOTHER Six months.

ANNIE Mum, you should / have told.

MOTHER Is it my turn now?

ANNIE What?

MOTHER I have a few questions I'd like to ask. If that's all right?

ANNIE –

Well... Sure.

MOTHER How is Mark?

ANNIE –

MOTHER Is he all right?

ANNIE Mark's gone.

MOTHER You or him?

ANNIE Him?

MOTHER Why?

ANNIE I think he got bored with me.

MOTHER Did you love him?

ANNIE Yes.

MOTHER Do you still love him?

ANNIE I do.

Very much.

MOTHER I'm sorry.

ANNIE Did you love Dad?

MOTHER I did. When I was younger.

ANNIE And later?

MOTHER We got used to each other.

ANNIE Did you ever think of leaving him?

MOTHER No.

ANNIE Do you think he ever thought of that?

MOTHER He left once. He was gone for almost a year.

ANNIE I didn't know.

MOTHER You were too young.

Do you like your job?

ANNIE I do.

Did you like yours?

MOTHER Never. I thought kids were always just a bit too loud.

Do you like living alone?

ANNIE No. Not at all.

Did you like Uncle George?

MOTHER I slept with him before he married your aunt.

ANNIE Mum.

MOTHER She doesn't know, so you better watch your mouth. All right?

ANNIE All right.

MOTHER Are you happy?

ANNIE No. Not right now.

Are you scared?

MOTHER No. Not any more.

Do you drink on your own?

ANNIE Sometimes I do.

MOTHER Why?

ANNIE If I think Mark is not coming back.

And since you died.

MOTHER Does it make you feel better?

ANNIE No. It makes me sick. Then I throw up.

Did you ever drink?

MOTHER Yes.

ANNIE On your own?

MOTHER Sometimes. When your dad was gone. And after you moved out.

ANNIE Did it make you feel better.

MOTHER For a moment. Yes.

ANNIE Did it hurt? You know. When you died?

MOTHER No.

ANNIE What did it feel like?

MOTHER It was new. Feeling I've never had before. First it felt like something got stuck in my throat. And it grew this time. And I couldn't cough it up.

–

It felt like it would take a while.

ANNIE Did it?

MOTHER Yes.

ANNIE How long?

MOTHER To me it seemed like hours.

ANNIE Did you know what it was?

Did you know you were dying?

MOTHER Yes. You know when it comes.

ANNIE Why didn't you call me?

MOTHER There was nothing you could've done.

ANNIE But if I hadn't left…you know, if I hadn't left the room, to make the tea.

MOTHER No. It was my time.

ANNIE –

I'm so sorry mum.

MOTHER You are still angry?

ANNIE Yes.

–

I think so.

MOTHER Who with?

ANNIE You. Mark. Dad. Myself. Everyone.

MOTHER What for?

ANNIE –

I don't know.

–

Were you angry?

MOTHER Oh yes.

ANNIE Who with?

MOTHER I don't know. Same. Everyone. Anyone.

ANNIE Why?

MOTHER For being old. I guess. And ill.

ANNIE What made you angry about it?

MOTHER I don't think I deserved it.

ANNIE I see.

MOTHER Do you think I did?

ANNIE No.

MOTHER Do you think it changed me?

ANNIE Yes.

MOTHER How?

ANNIE You became even angrier...you became mean.

MOTHER Did you wonder why?

ANNIE Sometimes.

MOTHER And? Did you ever find out?

ANNIE I think I did.

MOTHER So? Why?

ANNIE I'm still not sure.

It could've been all that waste and poison that couldn't leave your body.

MOTHER Or?

ANNIE Or – maybe you were always a bit selfish and mean and I just didn't notice it because – I'm your daughter and it's hard to notice those things in a parent.

MOTHER And?

Which do you think it was?

ANNIE –

MOTHER –

ANNIE I don't know.

–

Which one do you think it was?

MOTHER –

I don't know either.

It's been going on for too long.

ANNIE –

MOTHER –

DAD *(off)* Annie!

ANNIE I will have to go soon.

MOTHER I know.

ANNIE Can I get you anything before I go?

MOTHER No. I'm fine.

ANNIE Tea?

MOTHER No. Thank you.

ANNIE Sure?

MOTHER Yes.

ANNIE Okay. I better...

MOTHER ...

ANNIE I have to go and have breakfast.

MOTHER ...

ANNIE I think it might be ready.

MOTHER ...

ANNIE Dad's making it for me.

MOTHER ...

ANNIE I have to go.

    Voice from outside.

DAD Annie?

    MOTHER *doesn't move.*

DAD Annie!

    ANNIE *doesn't move.*

End

A PRAYER

AUTHOR'S NOTE

Between 2010 and 2015 directed by Lorne Campbell and Selma Dimitrijevic.

Creative Collaborator/Designer: Garance Marneur

Originally performed by Sandy Grierson at Northern Stage and Young Vic. At Hull Theatre and Northern Stage performed by Scott Turnbull. At the Almeida, Young Vic and caravan showcase performed by Elspeth Brodie.

In all versions God was played by the audience.

The original production of *A Prayer* was first co-commissioned and produced by Oran Mor as part of its A Play, A Pie and A Pint spring season 2010. The project was further developed at Northern Stage, Newcastle, after winning the Title Pending Award, the award for the most innovative, thoughtful, and intriguing proposal for a new piece of theatre.

This is the June 2011 draft. We expect the play will change with every actor that performs it. Hopefully it will change often and profoundly.

A Prayer was first produced by Greyscale on tour in 2009, directed by Lorne Campbell

CHARACTERS

M: Any gender, any age, any race.

M *is looking at God.*

God is looking at **M**.

How funny.

It feels as if the air is bit thinner, breathing is easier and things are clearer.

It feels confusingly joyous.

All sorts of thoughts are going through **M**'s *mind.*

Then **M** *does something.*

And then some more things go through **M**'s *mind.*

And then – after some time – **M** *speaks to God.*

M Hello.

If there is no answer, **M** *speaks again. It's not like he was expecting a reaction anyway.*

(Hello.)

If there is an answer, if God speaks back, it's almost too much for **M** *to take it.*

M *reacts to it and it takes him a few seconds to recover. Maybe a bit longer. Maybe much longer.*

God is still looking at him.

M *has never experienced this before.*

It's huge.

Sorry.

Pause.

*Things are going through **M**'s mind.*

I'm just a bit, mhmm, you know.

*Was **M** going to say "scared" or "too excited"?*

This is a bit weird.

M *looks carefully.*

It definitely is God.

Weird.

*God is looking at **M**. Patiently.*

Then suddenly, without any warning, all cynicism disappears just for a few moments.

It feels amazing. So, so good.

It's kind of dizzying in a good, calm way.

M *smiles. God probably smiles back.*

It doesn't last too long.

M *is not sure what just happened. He is not even sure that something happened.*

Does the feeling go away? Does it hang about for a while?

*On the other side of the room, **M** notices something. It's something he wants right now (like his glass of water and he really, really needs a sip now, or his towel if he just came out of the shower).*

He decides to go for it.

If I could just…

He goes towards the other side of the room.

Very carefully.

*If God moves out of his way, **M** thanks God.*

Thank you.

Not being able to turn his back to God, or to take his eyes off God, but not very comfortable about getting too close either.

If **M** *needs to get through God, he says things like:*

Excuse me.

I'll just, yes, thank you.

Eventually **M** *takes a sip / finds the towel / gets his clothes / does whatever else was he doing.*

M *is not sure what to do with God.*

Does he wait for a few moments for God to do something?

Okay, weird.

God doesn't do much.

Does **M** *wait for a few seconds?*

Are you going to say something?

Does God speak? Does God nod or give any other sign?

If God speaks, it's amazing and exciting.

M *was a bit more prepared for it this time.*

Okay.

Is **M** *confused about how God got in there?*

I thought I was maybe imagining...

you know...this.

Something.

But I'm not, am I?

Is **M** *saying this or asking a question? Does he know which one is it?*

You are here.

Is there any answer from God?

(Literally here.)

There is an answer, of some kind. A sign.

Really?

M *still needs the proof.*

He knows how he could get it but is not sure how to ask.

Would you mind if I check?

What's the best way to put this?

Can I touch you?

Does God give **M** *a sign?*

Okay.

M *is going to do it.*

Okay.

Here it is.

M *is getting closer to God.*

He is about to touch God.

This is pretty intense.

And...

M *touches God.*

Wow.

Fuck.

Wow.

God seems to be all right with this.

Fuck me/

sorry.

God doesn't seem to mind M *swearing. God even finds it amusing.*

Which was somewhat expected.

I just wanted to check.

Does checking seem ridiculous now?

Or does it make perfect sense?

What can M *do to say thank you for this, to return the favour?*

Do you want to touch me?

That seems only fair.

God gives M *a sign. Maybe God even says "Yes" out loud.* M *is getting slowly used to the voice of God.*

All right.

This is exciting.

Very exciting.

M *offers herself to be touched by God.*

God touches M.

Wow. *(Or some other non-sweary interjection)*

What is M*'s reaction? How big is his reaction? How does it feel?*

Okay.

Okay.

This was pretty huge. And weird.

I just wanted to make sure (that) you are really here.

Something.

And you are.

Something.

You see, the thing is, the thing is...

This is very, very confusing.

And pretty funny.

I never thought you are real.

That's true.

And now you seem to be here.

That seems true too.

And also – you don't look like, you don't really look like how...

Hmmmm.

I never imagined you would look like this.

Something.

I mean I never imagined you at all, but if I did, I would have imagined, something a bit more...

M *tries to describe what he means.*

But not...

Something.

Fuck me / sorry.

You see, I don't know how to – do this.

Something.

I mean, How did...

Where did you come from?

*Does God tell **M** where God came from? Is God telling the truth?*

*Did different parts of God come from different places. If yes. **M** can ask:*

I see.

That's weird.

So does that mean you can be in many places at the same time?

If God doesn't come from many places M *still thinks that's cool.*

That's cool.

M *enjoys this.*

And.

Do you always look like this?

Is there a simple yes or no answer?

Nice.

Something.

And do you…do this often?

God may be saying yes. God may be saying no. Either of those things might be a lie.

And do you know things, before they happen?

M *takes out a coin.*

Heads or tails?

God replies. God makes a choice.

M *flips the coin.*

Okay.

Something. God either got it right or not.

And can you

make things go…

(Sound for things being destroyed?)

you know

destroy them?

M *takes a biscuit/ a grape /something small and easily destructible and offers it to God to destroy.*

If you wanted to. Can you destroy this?

M *is inviting God to destroy it.*

What does God do?

Does God destroy it?

God probably does.

I see.

Something.

And how about about this?

M *puts something else in front of God for God to destroy it.*

An orange? Something a bit bigger but still easy to destroy.

Does God do it? Possibly.

M *continues putting more and more valuable things in front of God.*

Every time **M** *waits for God to destroy it before offering the next object.*

A bit of paper with a child's drawing on it? A book? Reading glasses? Debit card?

It might go on for a while...

But finally, after an offer from **M**, *God doesn't do anything.*

There is something God doesn't want to/can't destroy.

All right.

M feels like someone has just proved something, but he's not very clear on who or what.

All right.

Not – how I imagined you.

Not at all.

These revelations are very intriguing to M. *And quite exciting.*

And does it...

M removes what was left after God's last destruction and leaves the empty space in front of God.

Does it work

the other way

around?

Can you

M is not trying to outsmart God.

Can you make things, make something.

M is inviting God to create something.

Out of this?

What does God do?

Does God create something?

Does God even try?

Is God refusing to be tested like this?

One of those things happens.

And when it does it's obvious it's the only possible outcome.

Does it make **M** *laugh?*

There seems to be a strange understanding between **M** *and God at the moment. It makes them both feel pretty good. And pretty smart for some reason.*

Can you show me?

M *is even more comfortable, still probably wouldn't touch God casually but is not afraid to move any more.*

If God creates something or even if God says yes.

That's amazing. Really amazing.

So weird.

Something.

Because you see...

I don't really believe in God.

I never believed in you. Never.

Because, it doesn't / it didn't

it never seemed very – logical.

To me. It never seemed very – intelligent.

Does this offend God in any way?

I'm sorry about that.

Something.

But I was never ever told you might be this.

You seem kind and funny and sweet. And you wear nice shoes. And you laugh at things I say. And you seem to really listen to what I say.

From what I was told you are this huge and scary, and jealous, and stubborn, this manipulative and homophobic and petty and cruel thing.

Because that's what people say. The stories, that's what they make you sound like.

And I just thought I always thought, that doesn't sound very Godly.

No. That sounds Human.

M never put this into words before. He never thought he would.

Does it feel like he is finally talking to someone who might understand him?

Do you know what I mean?

M is not even contemplating how complex "do you know what I mean?" question might be. And he doesn't have to.

But now you are here I'm just confused, I'm not sure if you are

Is that what you, I mean

Are you stubborn?

What does God say to this?

(Are you) Jealous?

Does God reply?

Petty?

Cruel?

This is a bit much for M. How is his mind dealing with all this?

Okay.

This is a scary thought.

And, are you here to do something to me?

Something. If the answers is no that's a huge relief.

Okay, good. So are you here so I can do something for you?

Something.

Well I'm, not sure I can do much.

Something.

I mean, I don't really know how to pray.

No. (Sorry.)

I might remember a line or two of Our Father

But probably not in the right order

And I'm not sure if I can, you know, mean it.

So it doesn't seem worth doing it.

Really.

Is **M** *looking for clues from God? God is not giving him any clues at the moment.*

And I don't know any other prayers. You know, if you are not that God.

Oh, this is getting more and more complicated.

No, you are definitely not that God.

M *is genuinely asking these questions which are not questions.*

Now I know even less about what I can offer you.

Is **M** *going to try any of this?*

What about…

Something.

Do you want me to kneel for you?

God probably says yes or no. Does **M** *try?*

Shall I bow for you?

Okay.

Would you want me to hurt myself for you?

Something.

No, you don't look like that kind of God either.

You are actually…

M *looks carefully at God, he hasn't really noticed until now.*

You're actually quite pretty.

Is that **M** *flirting with God? God blushes.*

How about, would you want me to sing for you?

M *sings a song for God.*

Does God enjoy it? Does God join in?

Either way **M** *enjoys it.*

That was fun.

Something.

So God.

I guess people ask you for things a lot. Do they?

Do they?

Thought so.

I really don't want to take advantage of you in any way.

But I may never find myself in a position like this again, and there's something I would really like to know.

So. May I ask you a question?

Something.

Do you know what I'm talking about?

God probably doesn't. But then again you never know.

It is the strangest thing that ever happened to me.

Apart from this.

Something.

So... I'm in New York. In a hotel, on my own, I've never been there before.

And I couldn't sleep, the time was all wrong, it was too early, or maybe too late, and I was awake when I should have been asleep, so I went out.

Something.

I went out to this bar, this bar where they played jazz, and it wasn't like *The Carlyle* or anything like that, it was just a stupid little bar, where four guys played jazz, sitting on those funny high stools, and one of them holding the chubby guitar, and a few men…few people just sitting around because it was too late to go anywhere else.

So I walked in, I walked down, and sat at the bar, not looking around, looked past the barmen…

God might offer more details of the night, or correct M *about how it happened.*

A friendly guy, I looked to the row of bottles, whiskeys he had right next to the wall, and I ordered one.

And as he was taking the bottle down, I saw in the mirror behind the bottles, behind the barmen, behind the bar I saw a woman.

A woman looking straight at me. Seeing me looking at her. Definitely seeing me looking at her. And then she smiled.

Which was odd. Really odd.

Because women usually don't smile at me like that. Not if they don't know me and I'm sitting in a strange city and in a strange bar.

Something.

So I drank my whiskey. And then – I guess I was just curious – I ordered another one, and there she was. She was still looking at me.

So I turned around. And she smiled. And you know, I smiled.

And she said hello.

Hello.

And we started talking, and we talked all evening, all night.

And it was just easy.

It was at the same time the hardest and the easiest thing I've ever done, and it felt like we were doing it together and we knew how incredible, how unbelievable it is that this is how it feels to both of us.

It was just perfect.

Something.

And when it was time to leave the bar, she said she lived just around the corner and that I should come up. And I said yes.

It didn't feel dirty, it didn't feel cheap, it just – made sense. There was a logic, it was just so comfortable, so...nice.

We went up.

We talked all night.

We kissed.

We made love.

We talked some more.

And...

And laughed at how obvious it all is, you know.

How easy it is to talk, and we wondered why was...you know, what was all the fuss about. Men and women and trying to... when it seemed so easy, so ridiculously easy to us, just now.

We both knew it. And we both knew that the other one feels the same.

It was like...

God might offer what it was like. And God is absolutely right.

I woke up very early, because of the light, there was so much sun, sun and light coming into the room, and she was snoring, very gently, which was quite funny, but I didn't mind.

I knew this wasn't going to finish just like that, we were just about to start something. So quietly, very, very quietly I got up, got dressed, I got my wallet, and my jacket and went out to buy us coffee and croissants.

I was going to surprise her.

It was going to be a perfect morning. Because that's what made sense.

So I bought the coffee and croissants, four croissants, and then I bought flowers, which was a bit cheesy but I thought she would laugh, and I didn't really care much, because things were so perfect. Flowers made sense. I don't know. Somehow.

And I was on my way back, to this amazing women, I was just one block from her building, from where I spent the night, and then as I turned the corner... I looked up and...

God might sense what is coming next and offer it to **M**. *As before, God is absolutely right.*

...the building wasn't there.

It just wasn't there.

And I thought I got it wrong, so I went back, a few streets back, with my coffee, and flowers, and chocolate croissants and then tried again, going straight back to her building.

But it wasn't there.

I didn't know the town.

I've never been to New York before.

I know all that.

I could have taken the wrong turn.

...

But I didn't.

I knew where I spent the night.

I knew the building.

And it wasn't there.

Does God know what happened to the building?

So I went back, again and again…

I kept going back to the coffee shop and then again through the streets that should lead to her building but every time, every single time, I turned that corner, or eventually some other corner…it just…wasn't there.

And then I realised.

I know only her first name.

Nothing else.

I don't know where she works.

I don't know any of her friends.

I didn't know anything about her.

Except that her and I – make sense.

Something.

And then I realised she was going to wake up, she was going to wake up thinking she had this perfect night, with someone who feels the same, with someone who…gets her, she was going to wake up, just as I did, thinking this is just the beginning of something huge, of something real, and amazing, something she gave up a long time ago…and then she will realise I am not there.

She will think…it was a one-night stand for me.

She will think…it wasn't perfect. It wasn't easy.

She will think it was all a lie.

She will think I lied to her that night.

And I won't have a chance to tell her…that she is wrong.

How does **M** *go into asking the questions? What are the questions?*

So if you can, if you know those things,

…

if you can destroy things, and create things

Does **M** *mention things God destroyed or created just a few minutes ago?*

and have powers, and meet prayers...

if you have answers...

Something.

And you look like you do...you look so wise,

like you know so much about so many things.

If you do...can I just ask you.

Something.

(Do you think) I will...

will I ever meet her again?

(If I go back to New York?)

God answers **M**'s *question. It might be yes or no or something completely different bu* **M** *believes God knows the truth.*

If God says yes, **M** *has to ask:*

And will she, will she recognize me?

Does God say yes? If not does **M** *leave?*

And...

M *has to ask just this last question.*

...and will she know, that I am telling the truth, when I say I tried to find her, will she believe me...?

Something.

Will she believe me?

God gives **M** *an answer.*

And although huge, and odd, it feels good to know after all this time.

I see.

M *is grateful for it.*

M *is grateful to God for answering his question.*

Thank you.

Thank you.

The End

Gods Are Fallen And All Safety Gone

Property List

A comfortable chair and a few blankets (p1)

Small table (p1)

A few mugs, newspapers, glasses, TV schedule and a pair of socks scattered around the room (p1)

Cup of tea (p1)

A Prayer

Property List

On the other side of the room, M notices something. It's something he wants right now (like his glass of water and he really, really needs a sip now, or his towel if he just came out of the shower) (p44)

Eventually M takes a sip / finds the towel / gets his clothes / does whatever else he was doing (p44)

A coin (p50)

M takes a biscuit/ a grape /something small and easily destructible and offers it to God to destroy (p50)

M puts something else in front of God for God to destroy it. An orange? Something a bit bigger but still easy to destroy (p50)

M continues putting more and more valuable things in front of God (p50)

Every time M waits for God to destroy it before offering the next object (p50)

A bit of paper with a child's drawing on it? A book? Reading glasses? Debit card? (p50)

Lightning Source UK Ltd.
Milton Keynes UK
UKOW06f0052290416

273201UK00001B/26/P

9 780573 130113